KU-766-700

Wool

Annabelle Dixon

Photographs by Ed Barber

Contents

A & C Black · London

Is it made from wool?

These jumpers all look as if they are made from wool, but only one is really made from sheep's wool. Can you tell which one it is? (*The answer is on page 25.*)

The other jumpers are made from man-made fibres, such as nylon and acrylic. These fibres are made from oil, coal and wood.

Threads books in hardback

Beans	Plastics
Bread	Rice
Bricks	Rocks
Clay	Salt
Cotton	Silk
Eggs	Spices
Fruit	Tea
Glass	Water
Milk	Wood
Paper	Wool

First paperback edition 1992

First published 1988 in hardback by
A & C Black (Publishers) Limited
35 Bedford Row, London WC1R 4JH

ISBN 0–7136–3652–1

Copyright © 1992, 1988 A & C Black (Publishers) Ltd

A CIP catalogue record for this book
is available from the British Library.

Acknowledgements
Illustrations by Caroline Ewen
Photographs by Ed Barber, except for: p 3 (bottom), p 10, p 11,
p 15 (bottom), p 17 (right), p 23 (bottom) International Wool
Secretariat; p 8 (top) Ben Johnson; p 9 (sheep) British Wool
Marketing Board.

The author and publisher would like to thank the following
people whose help and co-operation made this book possible:
The staff and pupils at The Mayflower Primary School;
The Zoological Society of London; Vauxhall Urban Farm;
Elizabeth Hope and the pupils of Puller Memorial J.M.I. School;
Diane Pickover and the staff and pupils of St Andrew's J.M.I. School;
Penny Walsh; Lisa Collins; Hilary Auden.

Apart from any fair dealing for the purposes of research or private study, or
criticism or review, as permitted under the Copyright, Designs and Patents Act,
1988, this publication may be reproduced, stored or transmitted, in any form or
by any means, only with the prior permission in writing of the publishers, or in
the case of reprographic reproduction in accordance with the terms of the licences
issued by the Copyright Licensing Agency. Inquiries concerning reproduction
outside those terms should be sent to the publishers at the above named address.

Typeset by August Filmsetting, Haydock, St Helens
Printed in Belgium by Proost International Book Production

It is difficult to tell if something is made from sheep's wool just by looking at it. But you can often see if your guess was right by reading the labels on clothes or yarn.

Your label says acrylic.

This one's made from wool.

Look out for this special symbol on the labels. It is called the woolmark.

The woolmark symbol can only be used if something is made from pure new wool. The same symbol is used all over the world.

PURE NEW WOOL

3

If you can't find a label, you can do some tests to help you tell the difference between man-made fibres and wool.

First you will need to make a collection. Choose some things you think are made from sheep's wool and some you think are made from man-made fibres.

Here are some ideas

Old clothes
(such as a jumper, a scarf and some gloves)

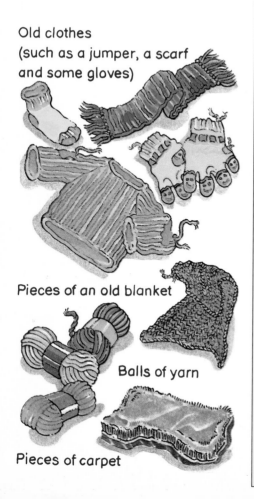

Pieces of an old blanket

Balls of yarn

Pieces of carpet

The feeling test

Feel all the things in your collection and brush them against your cheek.

Wool will feel soft, warm and bouncy.
Man-made fibres will feel flat and cool.

The pulling test

Cut a piece of yarn about as long as this page. Hold it at both ends and stretch it by pulling strongly. Then let go. What happens? Does the yarn spring back?

Wool will spring back however many times you do the test. But it will probably break more easily than man-made yarns. Man-made yarns will feel like string and go hard. They will not spring back as easily as wool.

The smelling test

Smell all the things in your collection. Some wools smell rather like fur.

Do they smell different when they are wet? Some people say that the smell of wet wool reminds them of wet dogs. Try doing this test blindfolded.

Turn over for some more tests.

The dampness test

You will need

One glove you think is made from **wool**

One glove you think is made from **man-made fibres**

Some water

A paper towel or a paper table napkin – a coloured one is best

A tablespoon

How to do it

1. Put on the gloves and sprinkle two tablespoons of water over each glove. Rub in the water and wait about five minutes. A wet woollen glove will feel warmer than a wet glove made from man-made fibres.

2. Take off both gloves and place them on the paper towel or napkin (wet side down). A woollen glove will not lose as much water as a glove made from man-made fibres.

The ice-cube test

You will need

One glove you think is made from wool

One glove you think is made from man-made fibres

Two small plastic bags

Twist ties

Ice-cubes

How to do it

1. Put some ice-cubes in each bag and close the bags tightly with the twist ties.

2. Put on the gloves and hold one bag in each hand.

Which ice-cubes melt first? Which hand feels cold first? Which glove would you prefer to wear when it is cold?

Now you know why wool is special. It always feels warm and soft and it is good at keeping out the cold. Wool can also get quite damp without feeling uncomfortable.

7

Where does wool come from?

Wool does not only come from sheep. All these animals have the kind of fur we call wool.

▼ We get mohair wool from this kind of goat.

▲ We get angora wool from this kind of rabbit. This one has just had its fur trimmed.

▼ We get vicuna wool from this animal.

All these wools are much more expensive than the wool we get from sheep. So most of our wool comes from sheep.

Wool from sheep

Blackface

There are many different kinds of sheep. Each kind of sheep has its own kind of wool. Look at the pictures of the wool from these three kinds of sheep. How many differences can you spot?

Dorset Horn

Black Welsh Mountain

Making things from wool

How is the wool from a sheep turned into your woollen jumper?

The first step is to cut the wool off the sheep. This feels rather like having a hair cut; it doesn't hurt the sheep. The wool is cut off in spring or summer when the sheep do not need their thick woollen coats to keep warm. They soon grow a new woollen coat.

A sheep's coat is called a fleece. It is cut off with special scissors called shears. Nowadays, the shears are usually electric, which makes the job faster and easier, but it's still hard work. It takes about five minutes to shear a sheep. A good sheep shearer can shear about 150 sheep in a day.

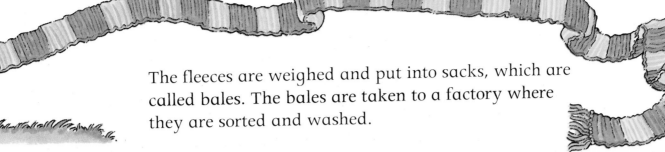

The fleeces are weighed and put into sacks, which are called bales. The bales are taken to a factory where they are sorted and washed.

If the fleeces were not washed, your jumper would have 8 tablespoonfuls of oil, a bag of weed seeds and half a bucketful of mud in it.

How to dye wool

Before fleeces are made into yarn, they are often dyed. Would you like to try this? Before you add any colour, you must do something to the wool which will stop the colour coming out in the wash.

You will need

Some raw sheep's wool or a ball of Aran wool

A deep pan (not aluminium)

A hot-plate or cooker
Ask an adult to help you with this.

100 g of alum
20 g of cream of tartar
These chemicals will 'fix' the colour.
They are called mordants.

How to do it

Fill the pan with cold water. Mix the alum and cream of tartar with a little water and stir this mixture into the pan. Heat the pan. When the water begins to get warm, add the wool.

Bring the water to the boil and simmer for 45 minutes. Then turn off the heat. When the water is cool, take out the wool. Do not rinse it. Keep it in a plastic bag so it will stay damp until you are ready to dye it.

You can buy tins of chemical dye or you can make your own dyes from plants.

To make yellow dye you will need

A large paper bag full of brown onion skins (This will make enough dye for about 250 grams of wool.)

A saucepan

An old spoon

or strainer

A hot-plate or cooker

How to do it

Boil up the onion skins in a deep pan full of water and simmer for two hours.

1. Turn off the heat and fish out the skins with the old spoon or strainer.

2. Put in the damp wool from the plastic bag and boil up the water again. Simmer for an hour.

Take the wool out of the pan and rinse it in clean, warm water. Leave the wool in a warm place to dry.

13

Carding wool

When the wool has been dyed, it has to be untangled before it can be made into yarn. Remember what you do to your hair after it has been washed? You brush or comb it so that the hairs all lie the same way. The same thing is done to wool. It is called carding the wool.

To card wool by hand, carders like these are used. In a factory, a machine uses hundreds of small combs to do the same job.

You can try carding wool with an ordinary comb or with two hair brushes. Lay the wool over one brush and pull the other brush over it. You should end up with a little ball of fluffy wool.

The carded wool is carefully rolled into a loose sausage shape. This is called a rolag or a sliver. The next job is to twist the rolag into a thread.

This picture of wool fibres was taken through a microscope. Can you see that each fibre has a rough, scaly edge? When wool fibres are twisted round each other, these rough scales lock on to each other and stop the fibres from pulling apart. This twisting is called spinning. *Turn over to see how to spin wool.*

How to spin wool

You can spin wool between your fingers but you will only be able to make lots of short lengths. These are not very useful for making things. To make long threads, you need something called a spindle.

To make a spindle you will need

A lump of plasticine about as big as a walnut

Animal wool (from a chemists) or a home-made rolag

A polystyrene meat tray

A short knitting needle about 15–20 cm long

① ② ③

How to do it

1. Place a cup or beaker over the tray and draw round it to make a circle. Cut out the circle.

2. Put the plasticine about 5 cm from the knob end of the needle and push the circle of polystyrene on top.

3. Twist some of your rolag into a thin thread and tie it between the plasticine and the knob of the needle. Tie it again about half way up the needle.

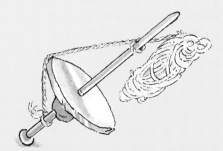

Twist your rolag between your fingers and let your spindle turn round. It should take the yarn with it and start to build up a ball of wool. It will take some practice to get this right.

◄ This is someone using a spindle to spin wool by hand.

▼ A spinning machine in a factory has hundreds of spindles. It works in a similar way to a hand spindle but the machines do the twisting.

◄ A spinning wheel is a kind of spindle. Can you work out why? What job is the foot doing? 17

Knitting

Find an old knitted jumper or scarf and make a cut in one end so you can pull a loose thread. Watch how the knitting comes undone. Can you see how the thread goes in and out of loops?

Go on pulling until all the knitting has disappeared. You should be left with one long piece of yarn. A whole jumper can be knitted from just one ball of yarn.

When wools of different colours are twisted round knitting needles, it's possible to make lots of different patterns. How many knitted patterns can you see round the edge of this page?

Large knitting needles are used for very thick, chunky wools. The smallest needles make very fine knitting. If you use one needle with a hook, it is called crocheting.

Knitting machines also use needles but they are different from the needles used for hand knitting. If you look carefully at this photograph you should be able to see lots of very small needles on the machine.

Weaving

Have you still got the collection you made earlier? If you have a piece of old blanket or a scarf, it may not be knitted. Cut off a piece of the blanket or scarf and pull a loose thread from one side. Does it look like this?

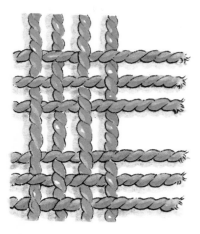

If the material has been woven, you should be able to see one set of threads which go up and down and one set of threads which go from side to side. The up-and-down threads are called warp threads. The side-to-side threads are called weft threads.

Warp threads

Weft threads

When people weave a piece of cloth, they set up the warp threads first. Then they weave the weft threads in and out of the warp threads. In the photograph, can you see that the weft thread is wound round a shuttle?

Try making your own loom

You will need

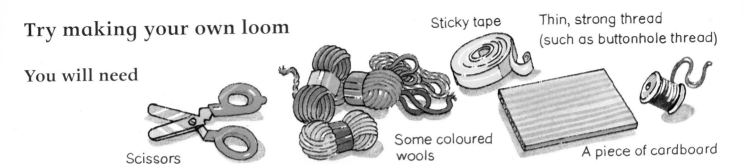

Scissors

Some coloured wools

Sticky tape

Thin, strong thread (such as buttonhole thread)

A piece of cardboard

How to do it

1. Cut a line of notches in the top and bottom edge of the piece of cardboard. Stick down one end of your warp thread and wind the rest of the thread round the card so it fits through the notches. Pull the thread as tight as you can. When you have finished, stick down the other end of the thread.

2. Now you can choose some different coloured yarns to weave in and out of the warp threads. You can use one long thread or lots of short threads.

21

Before you start weaving, it's a good idea to think of a pattern or a picture. Can you see the pattern behind the warp threads on this tapestry?

The pattern helps the weaver to remember where to start a different colour. Before you wind the warp threads around your loom, you could draw a pattern on the card. Make up some patterns like these.

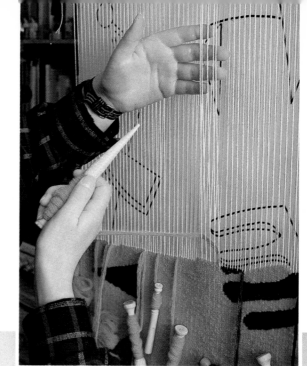

If you want to make a small mat, weave on one side of your loom.

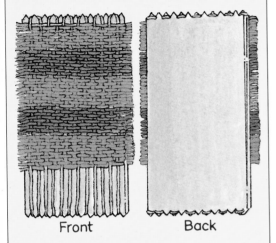

Front   Back

If you want to make a purse, you will have to weave all the way round your loom.

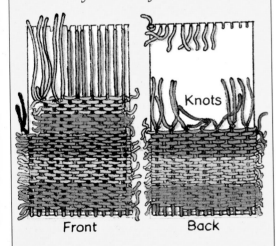

Knots

Front   Back

When you have finished, cut the threads so you can take out the cardboard. Tie a knot in the end of each thread so your weaving won't come undone.

People still weave by hand on simple looms. Can you see how this weaver lifts the warp threads on her loom?

Weaving machines in factories are more complicated than hand looms but they work in a similar way. 23

Woollen clothes

Next time you wear something made from wool, think about how it was made from a fleece like this one. Can you remember all the things that have to happen to the wool before it can be knitted or woven into clothes?

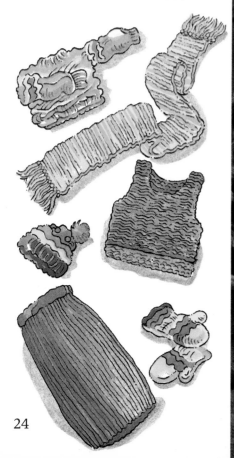

Wool is such a special fibre that even the best man-made fibres cannot copy it yet.

More things to do

1. Find out more about dyeing wool by making different coloured dyes from plants, fruits and vegetables. Try nettles, gooseberries, blackberries or red cabbage. Make up your own recipes or look in books about dyeing wool.

2. Try out this simple weaving pattern on your cardboard loom. (To see how to make a loom, look back at page 21.)
Line 1: over two threads; under one thread.
Line 2: under two threads; over one thread.
Use one colour for line 1 and a different colour for line 2.
Keep this two-line design going until you see a pattern coming.
You could make a book from your own weaving patterns and pictures of weaving from magazines or leaflets.

3. Collect some different coloured balls of wool and ask someone to teach you how to knit in plain stitch.
How to make a cushion cover
Knit some simple squares about 10cm long and 10cm wide.
Cut off a piece of wool and thread it through a large sewing needle. Sew the edges of the squares together but don't forget to leave one side open so you can put the cushion inside.
How to make a sleeveless top
Use large needles and thick wool to knit eight squares. Make each square about 20cm wide and 20cm long. Sew four of the squares together; then sew the other four squares together. Lay one block of squares on top of the other and sew them together across the shoulders and down the sides. Leave gaps for your head and arms to go through.

4. See if you can find out the answers to these questions.
Who were the first people to invent knitting?
What does a Guernsey jumper look like?
What kind of animal does Cashmere wool come from?
What patterns are knitted on Fair Isle jumpers?
How is felt made?

5. This book has told you about three kinds of sheep.
See if you can find out the names of some other kinds of sheep.
How long can you make your list?

Page 2 – answer: the jumper on the right is made from wool.

Index

(Numbers in **bold** type are pages which show activities.)